Shula Lewis

PEARLS OF WISDOM

PEARLS OF WISDOM

— Edited by —
WENDY WILSON

—Foreword by—
SHEILA HANCOCK

– Introduction by –
DEREK NUTTALL

Darton, Longman and Todd
London
Published in association with CRUSE

First published in Great Britain in 1988 by
Darton, Longman and Todd Ltd
89 Lillie Road
London SW6 1UD

in association with

CRUSE – Bereavement Care
Cruse House
126 Sheen Road
Richmond
Surrey TW9 1UR

British Library Cataloguing in Publication Data

Pearls of wisdom.
1. Quotations in English
I. Wilson, Wendy II. CRUSE
082

ISBN 0–232–51798–3

Phototypeset by Input Typesetting Ltd, London SW19 8DR
Printed in Great Britain by Anchor Brendon Ltd, Tiptree, Essex

CONTENTS

FOREWORD

I am an avid seeker after enlightenment. I cannot resist books with titles featuring words like 'love' and 'fear' that promise instant self-improvement. 'Wisdom' is another alluring bait. So this book is the answer to a soul-searching maiden's prayer, with the added bonus of discovering where the priorities of the famous lie.

For myself, I could not possibly place one pearl above another from my overflowing treasure chest of other people's wisdom, so I merely observe one of the many collected gems – 'A day at a time'.

By chance, on the day I was asked to write this Foreword, someone gave me a copy of the following poem, succinctly outlining my life-long quest for serenity, for which this precious book will provide many clues.

Autobiography in Five Short Chapters
by Portia Nelson

I I walk down the street
  There is a deep hole in the sidewalk.
  I fall in
  I am lost . . . I am helpless
  It isn't my fault.
 It takes forever to find a way out.

II I walk down the same street
There is a deep hole in the sidewalk.
I pretend I don't see it
I fall in again
I can't believe I am in the same place
But, it isn't my fault.
It still takes a long time to get out.

III I walk down the same street
There is a deep hole in the sidewalk.
I see it is there
I still fall in . . . it's a habit
My eyes are open
I know where I am
It is my fault.
I get out immediately.

IV I walk down the same street
There is a deep hole in the sidewalk.
I walk round it.

V I walk down another street.

SHEILA HANCOCK

INTRODUCTION
Thirty Years of Cruse

Since Cruse's formation in 1959 many thousands of people have found comfort and encouragement not only in the sensitive work of counsellors, advice on practical problems and in social mixing, but also through other people's words. Through the articulating and sharing of personal experiences with someone in a similar position; through reading of how others felt and coped. Talking of our loss, speaking our pain, is one way of slowly easing the burden and of finding our way through. Words, our own to others, others' to us, in times of special need are vehicles of expression, recovery and hope. It is fitting therefore that Wendy Wilson's idea of a 'Pearls of Wisdom' collection to mark Cruse's thirtieth year should come to fruition in this book. We are very grateful to her for compiling this anthology for Cruse, and to Darton, Longman and Todd for their collaboration in the publication.

When Cruse began the concern was for young widows with children. Soon all widows were included. The work widened to widowers in 1980 and now Cruse's help is available to all bereaved by death.

That help, available either through Cruse branches or Cruse headquarters consists of counselling, advice and information on practical issues and opportunities for social contact. Support and social groups are run, there is a wide range of specially written publications, and Cruse acts as a source of information on where additional help might be found.

Cruse runs training courses on bereavement counselling, conducts research into the special problems of bereavement and provides information on bereavement in response to an ever increasing number of enquiries from the United Kingdom and overseas.

Cruse's most significant contributions have come at both ends of the spectrum. By its very existence it has put bereavement on society's agenda, has helped others to think and talk about it. By speaking of grief itself it has freed others to do so, reducing the taboo. By its individual caring for those who seek its help it has shared pain, eased grief, alleviated loneliness and fostered recovery.

DEREK NUTTALL
Director of Cruse

PREFACE

All the royalties from the sale of this book will go to the national organisation Cruse – Bereavement Care, to mark its thirtieth or 'pearl' anniversary in 1989.

A host of well known and famous people have generously contributed their favourite quotations or words that have had a special significance or meaning for them. All these people have influenced and touched our lives in one way or another; whether it be through their writing, acting, faith, politics, products or sheer personality.

It is both fascinating and a privilege to know what has influenced them and what has been the philosophy that has helped to make them the people they are. In this book they have shared this with us through the magic and the power, the humour and the hope, the beauty and the poetry of words.

We know how much words help people who come to us at Cruse, people who are going through the loneliest loneliness of bereavement and learning to live without a loved one.

We know how much words help when our lives are shattered and shaken; and when we come to a crossroads and are not sure which way to turn. When we have to make difficult decisions we again seek refuge and understanding in words.

Words also help when we want to express our joy as well as our sorrow, our appreciation of life, our work, our conduct, our loves and friendships and moments of happiness and fulfilment.

Some find satisfaction and solace in writing and some find it in reading what others have so eloquently expressed. At difficult times how often have we felt much better after spilling out our thoughts and feelings on to paper. It has helped to clarify them and, once written, they are there for others to read and be helped; to feel they are not alone, that someone has been there before and understands. We all need yardsticks to live by, guidance from others that have trodden treacherous and difficult paths; and a sense of humour to keep us going.

Each individual contribution in this book could stand on its own. Together they form a rich and unique tapestry of thoughts: a string of pearls which it has been an honour and a pleasure to thread together.

I am very grateful to Sheila Hancock for her Foreword. Cruse is fortunate in having had her as a patron for many years. My personal thanks particularly go to Derek Nuttall and the staff at Cruse House, and to my family. All have given their unstinting encouragement and help – and put up with my constant name-dropping for many months. Warm appreciation is due to the authors, executors and publishers who have generously given their permission for the use of copyright poems and prose extracts.

My deepest gratitude goes to all the contributors for not only giving their support to Cruse but for sharing their values and, inevitably, part of themselves.

WENDY WILSON

FROM **Her Royal Highness The Duchess of Kent**

God give thee
Time for the task,
Wisdom for the work,
Grace for the way,
Love to the last.

ANON.

FROM **David Kossof**

Actor and author

'Keep always,' a wise man said, 'a dream in the pocket.'

'I am full of dreams,' said the young man.

'The one in the pocket should be unfulfilled,' said the wise man.

'And go,' he said, 'the way you are pushed. Don't struggle. Life will be richer. Recognise the push. Have courage.'

'I'll remember,' said the young man.

'Do not be afraid to show love,' said the wise man, 'or to weep. Or to ask a simple question.'

My late father said all of these things.

FROM **Dorothy Tutin**

Actress

I found this – but it belonged to Sue Ryder – very worth keeping around. I even stuck it on the fridge!

Think deeply
Speak gently
Love much
Laugh often
Work hard
Give freely
Pay promptly
Be kind.

ANON

But I like this for professional reasons:

Being an actress is like being a good sailor – No matter what ship she sails – in all conditions she must remain a good sailor!

ANTON CHEKHOV

FROM **Richard Briers**
Actor

This quotation by Henry Irving, the great Victorian actor, inspired and helped me to have the courage to take up the stage as a career.

First lay your lines; settle what you have to do and do it; the greater the opposition the more persevering and courageous you must be; if you are right and strength and life hold out, you must win.

HENRY IRVING

FROM **Lady Ryder of Warsaw**
Founder of the Sue Ryder Foundation

Many quotations come to mind but perhaps the one which I shall always treasure is 'Child of My Love'. The words are always with me, especially on my long drives.

Child of My love, fear not the unknown morrow,
Dread not the new demand life makes of thee
Thy ignorance doth hold no cause for sorrow
Since what thou knowest not is known to Me.

Thou canst not see today the hidden meaning
Of My command, but thou the light shalt gain
Walk on in faith, upon My promise leaning,
And as thou goest all shall be made plain.

One step thou seest – then go forward boldly,
One step is far enough for faith to see
Take that, and thy next duty shall be told thee,
For step by step thy Lord is leading thee.

Stand not in fear, thy adversaries counting,
Dare every peril, save to disobey

Thou shalt march on, all obstacles surmounting,
For I, the Strong, will open up the way.

Wherefore go gladly to the task assigned thee,
Having My promise, needing nothing more
Than just to know, where'ere the future find thee,
In all thy journeying I go before.

FRANK J. EXLEY

Child of My Love is also the title of Sue Ryder's autobiography.

FROM **Derek Nuttall**

Director of Cruse

In the Welsh Mabinogion is the story of a prince leading an army to free his sister. The forces fleeing from him cross a river and then break all the bridges. The prince, a giant of a man, laid himself across the river and his soldiers used him as their bridge. The story gives us the words

A fo ben bid bont –
He who would lead let him be a bridge

It was the motto of the Pantglas School in Aberfan, scene of the disaster in 1966 which killed 116 children and 28 adults. I was asked to go and work in Aberfan after the tragedy and remained there for seven years. This motto provided the inspiration for the logo adopted by the community of a bridge and flaming torch, symbolic of its reconciling work and the passing on of the experiences and lessons to others. The words remain for me as wise, inspiring and humbling for any who aspire to leadership.

FROM **Sir Edmund Hillary**

Mountaineer and now New Zealand High Commissioner to India

On many occasions I have used the following modest words which I like to feel epitomise the adventurous life.

Aim high! There is little virtue in easy victory.

FROM **Anna Massey**
Actress

Polonius' advice to Laertes has always meant a great deal to me.

This above all: to thine own self be true,
And it must follow, as the night the day,
Thou canst not then be false to any man.

WILLIAM SHAKESPEARE, *Hamlet*, Act 1 Scene 3

This passage was also chosen by **Joss Ackland** *who says:*

In any moment of crisis or decision-making, one tries to follow this example – though failing many times.

It is the most difficult challenge of all – the hardest to follow.

ALSO FROM **Joss Ackland**
Actor

There but for the grace of God go I.

adaptation from JOHN BRADFORD

FROM **Terry Scott**

Actor and comedian

This quotation is mine and is my philosophy of life.

I live with a fond eye on the past,
a shrewd eye on the future,
and my love for this very moment.

The explanation is to fondly smile at my past stupidity, fondly forgive my human frailties and wickedness, and to fondly smile at other people's unkindness to me – to live with a fond eye on the past.

To know that one can give too much of oneself, too much time, too much worry to the future. One must shrewdly assess the future, its changes, it excitements, its potential, and plan carefully and with as much intelligence as one can muster – to live with a shrewd eye on the future.

This moment I am alive. This moment is here to be lived, to be savoured, to be seen, to be felt and to be loved – my love is with this very moment.

FROM **Dame Jill Knight MP**

A Patron of Cruse

My favourite words are these and I have found them a yardstick to live by.

At the close of life the question is –
Not how much you have got,
But how much you have given.
Not how much you have won,
But how much you have done.
Not how much you have saved,
But how much you have sacrificed.
Not how much you were honoured,
But how much you have loved and served.

ANON.

FROM **The Earl of Lichfield**

Photographer

Go placidly amid the noise and haste, and remember what peace there may be in silence. As far as possible without surrender be on good terms with all persons. Speak your truth quietly and clearly; and listen to others, even the dull and ignorant; they too have their story. Avoid loud and aggressive persons, they are vexatious to the spirit. If you compare yourself with others, you may become vain and bitter; for always there will be greater and lesser persons than yourself. Enjoy your achievements as well as your plans. Keep interested in your own career, however humble; it is a real possession in the changing fortunes of time. Exercise caution in your business affairs; for the world is full of trickery. But let this not blind you to what virtue there is; many persons strive for high ideals; and everywhere life is full of heroism. Be yourself. Especially do not feign affection. Neither be cynical about love; for in the face of all aridity and disenchantment it is perennial as the grass. Take kindly the counsel of the years, gracefully surrendering the things of youth. Nurture strength of spirit to shield you in sudden misfortune. But do not distress yourself with imaginings. Many fears are born of fatigue and loneliness. Beyond a wholesome discipline, be gentle with yourself. You are a child of the universe, no less than the trees and the stars; you have a right to be here. And whether or not it is clear to you, no doubt the universe is unfolding as it should. Therefore be at peace with God, whatever you conceive Him to be, and whatever your labors and aspirations, in the noisy confusion of life keep peace with your soul. With all its sham, drudgery and broken dreams, it is still a beautiful world. Be cheerful. Strive to be happy.

Found in Old St Paul's Church,
Baltimore, dated 1692.

FROM **Terry Wogan**
Broadcaster and television personality

And the night will be filled with music,
And the cares that infest the day,
Shall fold their tents like the Arabs
And as silently steal away . . .

HENRY W. LONGFELLOW

FROM **Christina Foyle**

Managing Director of the world famous booksellers

The picture this brings is one of happiness, of the countryside, cool rivers, and everything that is so different from Charing Cross Road, where I spend most of my days.

Hearing this, Tseng Hsi put down his zither and rose to reply. 'My dream is a simple one. I would like it to be the end of springtime. I would like to be dressed in light fresh clothes. Then I would like to go with some friends and swim in the river Yi and cool in the spring breezes. After we had swum for a while, I dream of returning slowly home, talking and singing along the way.

Confucius looked at Tseng Hsi for a moment, then smiled. 'You know, all the dreams I have heard have merit. But if I were to choose myself to accompany one of you, it would be you, Tseng Hsi.'

CONFUCIUS

FROM **Roger Royle**

Religious broadcaster

For all that has been – thanks
To all that shall be – yes.

DAG HAMMARSKJÖLD

Dag Hammarskjöld who died in 1961 was the Secretary-General of the United Nations and, after his death, a collection of his sayings was found and they have been put into a book called 'Markings'. Why I like that quote so much is that it is so positive. It is so easy to be negative about many things today, but with a saying like that, you can't but be positive. I think it is a saying that must be of encouragement to anyone, even going through the darkest of days.

FROM **Marjorie Proops**

Advice columnist

I once had a letter from a distraught wife, begging me to tell her how she could stop her husband snoring. 'Sometimes,' she wrote, 'I feel like putting a pillow over his face!'

I offered a few suggestions and then, a year or so later, she wrote again, telling me her beloved husband had died. 'What wouldn't I give now,' she said, 'to have him beside me in bed, snoring . . .'

FROM **Antony Hopkins**

Composer and conductor

In the belief that Nature abhors a vacuum I have always maintained that if the brain is kept empty, creative thoughts will rush in to fill the space; consequently I virtually never remember quotations. There is however one exception which I do find myself repeating from time to time. It comes from W. H. Hudson's autobiography 'Far Away and Long Ago' and from which I know one paragraph through Michael Tippett's wonderful setting for tenor and piano, 'Boyhood's End'. The sentence summons up memories of Hudson's childhood, but I use it to reflect on various episodes in my own life.

What then did I want?
What did I ask to have?
If the question had been put to me then,
and if I had been capable of expressing
what was in me, I should have replied:
I want only to keep what I have.

W. H. HUDSON

FROM **The Rt. Hon. David Steel MP**

James Hogg was a poet from the Borders region of Scotland and was known as the Ettrick Shepherd. What I like about this quotation is that it succinctly shows man's error in desperately seeking perfection in others, and how much better it is to look at our fellow men with compassion and tolerance. I believe many of the world's troubles would be solved if we all took this attitude.

How foolish of mankind to look for perfection
In any poor changeling under the sun!
By nature, or habit, or want of reflection,
To vices or folly we heedlessly run.
The man who is modest and kind in his nature,
And open and cheerful in every degree;
Who feels for the woes of his own fellow creature,
Though subject to failings, is dear unto me.

JAMES HOGG

FROM **Sir John Harvey-Jones**
former Chairman of ICI

In my business life I have found this precept has been of most personal assistance to me.

The best is the enemy of the good.

VOLTAIRE

FROM **Sir Harry Secombe**

Actor, comedian and singer

One of my favourite sayings, which I have always found remarkably accurate is:

Always judge a person by the way they treat someone who can be of no possible use to them.

FROM **Susannah York**
Actress

I pass through this world but once: any kindness I can do therefore let me do it now.

attributed to ETIENNE DE GRELLET

I found this written in Gothic script on the oak beams of the chapel of the house where I grew up.

The words had been painted over, but after long scrutiny (three or four weeks!) through magnifying glasses and binoculars they gradually became discernible.

FROM **The Rt. Hon. Margaret Thatcher MP**
Prime Minister

Life is not made up of great sacrifices and duties but of little things: in which smiles and kindness given habitually are what win and preserve the heart and secure comfort.

SIR HUMPHREY DAVY

FROM **Sir Sigmund Sternberg**
Honorary Treasurer of Cruse

When Death summons a man to appear before his Creator, three friends are his: The first, whom he loves most, is money, but money cannot accompany him one step: his second friend is relatives, but they can only accompany him to the grave, and cannot defend him before the Judge. It is his third friend, whom he does not highly esteem, his good deeds, who can go with him, and can appear before the King, and can obtain his acquittal.

adaptation from RABBI ELIEZER

FROM **Morris West**

Novelist

It must be considered that there is nothing more difficult to carry out, nor more doubtful of success, nor more dangerous to handle, than to initiate a new order of things. For a reformer has enemies in all those who profit by the old order, and only lukewarm defenders in all those who would profit by the new.

MACHIAVELLI

FROM **Peter Ustinov**

Actor, dramatist and film director

One of my favourite quotations is:

If success had a form envy would be its shadow.

attributed to SENECA

FROM **The Rt. Hon. Nigel Lawson MP**
Chancellor of the Exchequer

I have chosen the following because it provides some justification for my own career.

There are now in this country, we may say, but two modes left in which an individual mind can hope to produce much direct effect upon the minds and destinies of his Countrymen generally; as a Member of Parliament, or an Editor of a London newspaper.

In both these capacities much may still be done by an individual because, while the power of the collective body is very great, the number of participants in it does not admit of much increase.

JOHN STUART MILL

FROM **Admiral of the Fleet Sir John Fieldhouse**
Chief of the Defence Staff 1985–8

This offering is my motive for delegation!

Indispensable Man

Some day when you're feeling important –
Some day when your ego's in bloom,
Some day when you take it for granted
You're the best-qualified man in the room –
Take a bucket and fill it with water,
Put your hands in it, up to the wrist,
Pull them out and the hole that remains
Is a measure of *how* you'll be missed!
The moral of this is quite simple,
You must do the best that you can.
Be proud of yourself – but remember!
There is *no* indispensable man.

ANON.

FROM **The Most Revd Desmond M. Tutu**
Anglican Archbishop of Cape Town

While we were yet sinners Christ died for us.

ROM. 5:8

This is my favourite quotation because I realise more and more every day that God loves me not because I am lovable: I am lovable because he loves me.

His love for me precedes any achievement on my part. It is all of grace. This speaks volumes about my value and that of other human beings – our worth in the sight of God is intrinsic to who we are. It does not depend on any extraneous thing.

Consequently EVERY human being is of immense, of infinite value. This truth is subversive of all injustice, oppression and exploitation. Isn't it tremendous? And NOTHING can change God's love for me, because God does not change.

FROM **The Rt. Revd Richard Harries**
Bishop of Oxford

This Jack, joke poor potsherd, patch, matchwood, immortal diamond,
Is immortal diamond.

GERARD MANLEY HOPKINS

These lines describe a human being from many points of view. From so many points of view we are nothing at all. Yet at the same time we are immortal diamonds. I like the way the poet brings out the fact that we are both of no worth at all and yet of infinite worth.

FROM **Bryan Gould MP**

No man is an Island, entire of it self; every man is a piece of the Continent, a part of the main; if a clod be washed away by the sea, Europe is the less, as well as if a promontory were, as well as if a manor of thy friends or of thine own were; any man's death diminishes me, because I am involved in Mankind; And therefore never send to know for whom the bell tolls; it tolls for thee.

JOHN DONNE

FROM **Glenda Jackson**

Actress and a Patron of Cruse

Only Connect.

E. M. FORSTER

FROM **Ted Hughes**
Poet Laureate

I think I could turn and live with animals, they are so placid
and self contained;
I stand and look at them long and long.
They do not sweat and whine about their condition;
They do not lie awake in the dark and weep for their sins;
They do not make me sick discussing their duty to God;
Not one is dissatisfied – not one is demented with the mania
of owning things;
Not one kneels to another, nor to his kind that lived thousands
of years ago;
Not one is respectable or industrious over the whole earth.

WALT WHITMAN

Walt Whitman is not saying he would like to become an animal, but that he would like to live with them, among them, near them. He did not know what we now know: that the companionship of animals helps us in many ways, reduces suffering and prolongs life. It is a curious fact. And it is a curious question, why they should have this effect on us. Maybe these lines of Whitman's, which are among the most famous he ever wrote, appeal so strongly because they help to answer that question, and supply the words for what we instinctively know and need to remember often.

FROM **Kingsley Amis**
Author and a Patron of Cruse

Everything is what it is, and not another thing.

JOSEPH BUTLER

Butler intended this more as an objection to platonic idealism, but I have always interpreted it, and found it helpful, as a reminder that we must call things by their right names, that, for example, kindness is kindness and not a manifestation of a guilty conscience, and stupidity is stupidity and not the result of educational deprivation or bad housing.

FROM **John Mortimer**

Barrister, playwright and author

These words should be written in gold over every judge's chair and in every government office. Anyone can believe in free speech for thoughts they agree with; the test of democracy is our tolerance of views we may find repulsive. At a time when free speech is under threat in this country this is my most important quotation.

I disapprove of what you say, but I will defend to the death your right to say it.

attributed to VOLTAIRE

FROM **The Rt. Hon. Denis Healey MP**

Men are asked for freedom of speech. God gave them freedom of thought, but they do not use it.

SØREN KIERKEGAARD

FROM **Catherine Cookson**
Author

For many years now I have been helped both spiritually and physically by attending to the saying:

The kingdom of God is within you.

LUKE 17:21

but it is up to oneself to open the door.

FROM **Jean Coggan**

Writer and wife of Lord Coggan, the former Archbishop of Canterbury

I was busy in the little kitchen of our holiday cottage in Yorkshire. I was very hot and bothered, hurrying to get a meal ready on time. Suddenly a voice seemed to whisper:

Listen to the song God is singing for you.

I did so and immediately I heard the music of the little babbling stream which trickled over the stones through the garden.

How often in the rush of life it is necessary to stop what one is doing; to open one's whole self to listen to what God is saying. His song refreshes, restores and steadies the heart and mind.

FROM **Dame Cicely Saunders**
Founder of the Hospice Movement

These were the words which directed me to begin planning a modern hospice, committed to care, research and teaching. Over and over again regular reading brought its encouragement back to mind in the eight years before the hospice finally opened to receive its first patients.

For me it has given confidence that while constant learning by listening to patients and their families will show a way ahead, there is a love and power greater than mine that will use me and many others in bringing it to pass.

Commit thy way unto the Lord; trust also in him; and he shall bring it to pass.

Ps. 37:5

FROM **Charlotte Lessing**
former Editor-in-Chief of Good Housekeeping Magazine

My guiding philosophy is Shakespeare's

To thine own self be true.

Hamlet, Act 1 Scene 3

When in doubt this comes into my mind at many times.

On a more practical/business side, I have always followed the maxim:

Advance with courage.

ANON.

It has been very important to me in both private and public life. When in doubt I have always said this to myself and gone full steam ahead. Obviously I have made mistakes but things I haven't done I have regretted more than things I have done.

FROM **Jeffrey Archer**
Author

The heights by great men reached and kept
Were not attained by sudden flight
But they, while their companions slept
Were toiling upward in the night.

HENRY W. LONGFELLOW

FROM **Dr Miriam Stoppard**
Writer and broadcaster

This quotation is a favourite of mine as it is from my husband.

All you have to march to is the beat of your own drum so march to that.

TOM STOPPARD

FROM **The Hon. Greville Janner QC, MP**

A Patron of Cruse

My parents taught me to look forward and not back. We do not tread the same path twice and we must make the best of that which we cannot change.

The moving Finger writes; and having writ
Moves on: Nor all your Piety nor Wit
shall lure it back to cancel half a Line,
nor all thy Tears wash out a Word of it.

EDWARD FITZGERALD from *The Rubáiyát of Omar Khayyám*

FROM **The Most Revd and Rt. Hon. Robert Runcie**
Archbishop of Canterbury

On a February evening in 1987, Irina Ratushinskaya most kindly came and read some of her poems in our chapel at Lambeth. She had recently been released from a corrective labour colony in Russia. She had been there for most of the time since her arrest in 1982. Despite all she had suffered, she was supremely calm and strong. I could see that this strength and confidence had grown to a large extent from her sufferings. And from her ability to express her pain: and the stubborn hope which shines through all her prison poems. Here is my favourite:

O Lord, what shall I say

O Lord, what shall I say that hasn't been said before?
Here I am under Your wind in my canvas clothes,
Between Your breathing and the midnight plague –
O my Lord!

What shall I say at Your interrogation, if I'm ordered
Not to be silent, but to turn and face my country –
With its deadly amusements, its rags of parting, deaf and
  dumb –
O my Lord!

How will You dare to judge,
According to what tribunal?
What will You answer, when I force my way through and
  arrive –
When I stand up and lean my shoulder against the glass
  partition –
And look at You
And ask You about nothing.

IRINA RATUSHINSKAYA

FROM **Dame Judi Dench**

Actress

I find the following quotation very helpful to recall during times of stress or whenever I feel things are getting on top of me.

There's a special providence in the fall of a sparrow. If it be now, 'tis not to come; if it be not to come, it will be now; if it be not now, yet it will come: the readiness is all. Since no man, of aught he leaves, knows what is't to leave betimes, let be.

WILLIAM SHAKESPEARE, *Hamlet*, Act 5 Scene 2

FROM **The Rt. Hon. Douglas Hurd MP**
Home Secretary

I would like to contribute:

> God imparteth by the way
> Strength sufficient for the day.
>
> J. E. SAXBY

This was a verse put through our letter box by our neighbour in Oxfordshire the day after I was appointed Secretary of State for Northern Ireland. It meant a great deal, then and now, because it is absolutely true. Somehow one does *get extra strength and courage to deal with difficult tasks.*

I discovered that it came from a verse by J. E. Saxby in a small book published in 1890 called 'Daily Strength for Daily Needs', intended, as the preface says, as a daily companion and counsellor. It is full of wise words.

FROM **Claire Rayner**

Writer and broadcaster

When I was quite young, my grandmother taught me a Chinese proverb – or so she said it was – which had to be said aloud at all times of stress both good and bad. When everything was awful, dreadful or depressing you must use the phrase; when everything was wonderful and glorious and exciting you were to use the phrase. When everything was dreary, dull and boring you were to use the phrase – in fact you should say it at least once a day!

And the phrase? Just four words:

This too will pass.

ANON.

And my grandmother was right. I've used the phrase many, many times (if not every day!) and it never fails to get my wheels back on the rails.

FROM **Rabbi Julia Neuberger**

Writer and broadcaster

When I was particularly depressed in my early years of studying Hebrew at Cambridge – before becoming a rabbi – at the nature of negative attitudes to women in Judaism, I found the following in a midrash (rabbinic commentary), which dates from approximately the tenth century.

It matters not whether a person be Jew or Gentile, male or female, free person or slave – it is according to his deeds that the Holy Spirit rests upon an individual.

SEDER ELIYYAHU RABBA

FROM **The Rt. Hon. Neil Kinnock MP**
Leader of Her Majesty's Opposition

Let us have faith that right makes might; and in that faith let us to that end dare to do our duty as we understand it.

ABRAHAM LINCOLN

FROM **The Rt. Hon. the Lord Mackay of Clashfern**
Lord Chancellor

A favourite quotation is:

If any of you lack wisdom, let him ask of God, that giveth to all men liberally and upbraideth not; and it shall be given him.

JAS. 1:5

This verse has often encouraged me in prayer when I have been faced with difficult decisions or hard tasks.

I do not know a better way to seek or obtain a pearl of wisdom.

FROM **Frank Muir**

Author and broadcaster

The wisest advice I know was given to me by my great-great-grandmother, a wonderful old lady, ninety-four and not one grey hair on her head (she was completely bald). She looked me in the eye, patted me on the head and said 'Rover,' (her eyesight was still good but her memory was lapsing, poor dear), 'Rover,' she said, 'however successful you become in life, which is highly unlikely considering how close together your eyes are':

Always give a thought to those unfortunates who are unfortunately not so fortunate as those who are fortunate enough to be more fortunate than those less fortunate than themselves. Or would you rather be a fish?

FROM **Cleo Laine**
Vocalist

When I feel as if the world owes me a living, or someone has been hurtful, I tell myself this little verse, which always seems to help, because it makes me laugh. And it's true too!

Life ain't all ya want, but it's all ya got, so have it.
Stick a geranium in your hat and be happy.

FROM **Sir Hugh Casson**

Architect and former President of the Royal Academy

Favourite quotations come and go according to age and circumstance. I still, however, believe in the perceptive wisdom of a remark by John Ruskin – artist, critic and radical reformer – who said:

Art is part of life or it is nothing.

JOHN RUSKIN

that is, it is not icing on the cake nor the investment hobby of the wealthy nor the private playground of pundits speaking and writing in their own hallucinatory jargon, but something to be practised and enjoyed at all levels, and at every age.

FROM **Bernat Klein**

Designer and Artist

I have found, both as a designer and as an individual interested in the Visual Arts, these words an invaluable guide in determining the validity of work which I have looked at over the years.

The function of Art is not to reflect the visible but to make the invisible visible.

PAUL KLEE

FROM **Roald Dahl**
Writer

All art is a lie to which we give the semblance of truth.

E. DEGAS

FROM **David Hicks**

Interior Designer

In my design work all through my career I have concentrated on simple design solutions and on understatement, and I have always avoided vulgarity. The four quotations below sum this up.

Simplicity and naturalness are the truest marks of distinction.

W. SOMERSET MAUGHAM

There is a majesty in simplicity.

ALEXANDER POPE

Simplicity is an exact medium between too little and too much.

SIR JOSHUA REYNOLDS

Less is more.

ROBERT BROWNING

FROM **Edna O'Brien**
Writer

I don't know where I read this but I thought it so funny I copied it into my journal and read it whenever I cook for hordes of people, because by being reminded of Lady B's plight, I somehow can temper my own.

'A cook – a cook. What is a cook?' Last coherent words of Lady B before she suffered a nervous breakdown.

ANON.

FROM **Rabbi Lionel Blue**
Writer and broadcaster

Lionel Blue sends us these lines from his book 'Bolts from the Blue'.

A fallen soufflé is just a risen omelette. It depends on how you look at it, that's all – from above or below.

FROM **Prue Leith**
Cookery expert

I am an inveterate chatterbox and I need this cruel truth to keep me from blow-by-blow chapter and verse.

Le secret d'ennuyer c'est tout dire.
(The secret of being a bore is to tell all.)

FRENCH PROVERB

Another quotation I have found invaluable is:

Thy friend has a friend, and thy friend's friend has a friend. Be discreet.

YIDDISH FOLK SAYING

I have seen so many people get into trouble, just by talking too much.

FROM **Norris McWhirter**
Author, publisher and broadcaster

Secondhand car salesmen are usually cited as the sort of people with whom it is always unwise to do business. In the 1950s the team manager of the British athletics team was the famous Jack Crump of Surrey. He used to dispense advice freely. I have always remembered one sage piece he was fond of giving to members of the team:

Never forget, anyone who will twist his own wife will twist anyone else.

JACK CRUMP

One wonders over the years how many disasters he was instrumental in averting.

FROM **Norman Willis**

General Secretary of the TUC

Have faith in Allah, but always tie your camel up.

THE KORAN

This was used by me at a special Trades Union Congress as an Arab proverb taken from the BBC programme 'It Ain't 'Arf 'Ot Mum'. An overseas delegate later told me that it is from the Koran.

I also like the following by William Sinclair who was an eighteenth-century Renfrewshire philosopher:

It is better by far to be within one Scots mile of where you were making for than on the exact spot of somewhere else.

WILLIAM SINCLAIR

FROM **Ernie Wise**

Comedian

My mother came out with many words of wisdom. From these statements you can gather we were on a tight budget!

Your bank book is your best friend.

Spend a little, save a little.

When there is no money in the house love flies out of the window.

FROM **Henry Cooper**

Sports and television personality

When in the boxing ring my thoughts were:

When in doubt – stick your left out.

FROM **Sir Cyril Smith MP**
A Patron of Cruse

It's not the size of the dog in the fight that matters, but the size of the fight in the dog.

ANON.

FROM **Richard Baker**

Broadcaster and author

I was very struck recently by a critical remark by Rosalie Colie apropos of 'The Praise of Folly' by Erasmus. She wrote:

Making mistakes serves man well, since his salvation depends upon realisation of his own folly.

ROSALIE COLIE

As an inveterate mistake-maker, I was rather comforted by this assertion!

FROM **Richard Adams**

Author

These words are from Dr Johnson, one of my three great heroes, the other two being Shakespeare and Jane Austen.

Boswell: 'So, Sir, you laugh at schemes of political improvement.'

Johnson: 'Why, Sir, most schemes of political improvement are very laughable things.'

SAMUEL JOHNSON

FROM **Michael Aspel**

Broadcaster and writer

I can't remember where or when I came across this quotation but I appreciated its irony, particularly when I was facing some major surgery. The surgeon was amused too.

God and the Doctor we alike adore
But only when in danger, not before;
The danger o'er, both are alike requited,
God is forgotten and the Doctor slighted.

JOHN OWEN

FROM **Dr Colin Murray Parkes**

Senior Lecturer in Psychiatry and Chairman of Cruse

Something is afoot in the universe, some issue is at stake, which cannot be better described than as a period of gestation and birth; the birth of the spiritual reality formed by the souls of men and the matter which they bear along with them . . .

The world, looked at empirically on our scale, is an immense groping, an immense search, an immense attack; it can only progress at the cost of many failures and casualities. The sufferers, whatever the nature of their suffering, are the reflection of this austere but noble condition. They are not useless and diminished elements. They are merely those who pay the price of universal progress and triumph. They are the ones who have fallen on the field of honour.

TEILHARD DE CHARDIN

The truth I am trying to grasp is the grasp that is trying to
grasp it.
I have seen the Bird of Paradise,
she has spread herself before me,
and I shall never be the same again.
There is nothing to be afraid of. Nothing.

Exactly.

The life I am trying to grasp is the me that is trying to grasp
it.

R. D. LAING

FROM **Patrick Moore**

Astronomer, author and broadcaster

I will go for Sherlock Holmes:

When you have eliminated the impossible, whatever remains, however improbable, must be the truth.

SIR ARTHUR CONAN DOYLE

It is so true in astronomy, as in everything else. Could anything be more improbable than a Black Hole? But it is not impossible; so it must be true!

FROM **The Hon. David Sieff**
Director of Marks and Spencer

A quotation which is part of my family's, and Marks and Spencer's, history is:

Don't Ask the Price Its a Penny.

And the following is a section of the Sieff family motto:

Without knowledge there is no understanding;
without understanding there is no knowledge.

FROM **The Rt. Hon. Sir Geoffrey Howe QC, MP**
Foreign Secretary

Now it is a terrible business to mark a man out for the vengeance of men. But it is a thing to which a man can grow accustomed, as he can to other terrible things; he can even grow accustomed to the sun. And the horrible thing about all legal officials, even the best, about all Judges, Magistrates, Barristers, Detectives, and Policemen, is not that they are wicked (some of them are good), not that they are stupid (several of them are quite intelligent), it is simply that they have got used to it. Strictly they do not see the prisoner in the dock; all they see is the usual man in the usual place. They do not see the awful Court of Judgment; they only see their own workshop.

G. K. CHESTERTON

I originally found this an impressively useful reminder, in the days when I practised at the Bar, and sat as Deputy Chairman of Quarter Sessions, of the need to avoid behaving as though you are dealing with 'the usual man in the usual place'.

But the same lesson is equally true for every job or profession.

FROM **The Rt. Revd David Sheppard**
Bishop of Liverpool

I call you servants no longer; a servant does not know what his master is about. I have called you friends, because I have disclosed to you everything that I heard from my Father. You did not choose me: I chose you.

JOHN 15:15–16

This text has long expressed for me the heart of the Christian experience. Instead of a code of laws or rules, which a servant might receive from a distant master, the Christian is treated as a friend, taken into the Lord's confidence and called to act as his responsible partner in His continuing creation.

On the morning of St Barnabas day 1975, when I was to be installed later in the day as Bishop of Liverpool, the gospel reading at the Eucharist included these words. Faced with such a daunting task, there was great encouragement in hearing the words, 'You did not choose me: I chose you.'

FROM **Julian Lloyd Webber**
Cellist

I am delighted to contribute one of my favourite quotations.

If God be for us, who can be against us?

ROM. 8:31

FROM **Mother Frances Dominica**

Helen House Hospice for Children

I have chosen this extract from 'Mister God, This is Anna' as it seems to me to be self explanatory!

'Fynn you can love better than any people that ever was, and so can I, can't I? But Mister God is different. You see, Fynn, people can only love outside and can only kiss outside, but Mister God can love you right inside, and Mister God can kiss you right inside, so it's different. Mister God ain't like us; we are a little bit like Mister God, but not much yet.

'You see, Fynn, Mister God is different from us because he can finish things and we can't. I can't finish loving you because I shall be dead millions of years before I can finish, but Mister God can finish loving you, and so it's not the same kind of love, is it?'

FYNN

FROM **Dr Dora Black**

Consultant Child Psychiatrist and Vice-Chairman of Cruse

The following quotes about children I often find myself using to parents who are troubled about their relationship with their child.

The apple doesn't fall far from the tree.

AMERICAN PROVERB

The most important thing that parents can do for their children is to survive their childhood.

DR KENNETH CAMERON

Dr Cameron was formerly Consultant Child Psychiatrist at the Maudsley Hospital, and he taught me child psychiatry.

Your children are not your children.
They are the sons and daughters of life's longing for itself.
They come through you but are not from you,
And though they are with you yet they belong not to you.

You may give them your love but not your thoughts,
For they have their own thoughts.
You may house their bodies but not their souls,
For their souls dwell in the house of tomorrow
Which you cannot visit, not even in your dreams.

You may strive to be like them,
But seek not to make them like you.
For life goes not backwards nor tarries with yesterday.
You are the bows from which your children as living arrows
are set forth.

KAHLIL GIBRAN

Also from **Richard Adams**

I am sure that neither death, nor life, nor angels, nor principalities, nor things present, nor things to come, nor powers, nor height, nor depth, nor anything else in all creation, will be able to separate us from the love of God in Christ Jesus our Lord.

ROM. 8:38–39

FROM **Dame Daphne du Maurier**
Writer

Daphne du Maurier, now in her eighties, has, she says 'retired from writing' but sends the following words of comfort to those who have lost a spouse. They were first written after the death of her own husband.

I would say to those who mourn – and I can only speak from my own experience – look upon each day that comes as a challenge, as a test of courage. The pain will come in waves, some days worse than others, for no apparent reason. Accept the pain. Do not suppress it. Never attempt to hide grief from yourself. Little by little, just as the deaf, the blind, the handicapped develop with time an extra sense to balance disability, so the bereaved, the widowed, will find new strength, new vision, born of the very pain and loneliness which seem, at first, impossible to master.

I remember on our wedding day, in July 1932, the good priest who married us drawing a comparison between the little boat in which we were to set forth on our honeymoon and marriage itself. 'You will embark,' he said, 'on a fair sea, and at times there will be fair weather, but not always. You will meet storms and overcome them. You will take it in turns to steer your boat through fair weather and foul. Never lose courage. Safe harbour awaits you both in the end.'

Today I remember this advice with gratitude. Even if I must, of necessity, steer my boat alone, I shall not, so I trust, lose my bearings but, because of all I have learnt through the past three-and-thirty years, with my fellow helmsman at my side, come eventually to my journey's end.

DAPHNE DU MAURIER

FROM **Mary Stott**
Writer and journalist

Everyone who has suffered the loss of a beloved lifetime partner inevitably thinks from time to time, perhaps quite often, of the implications of dying and of death itself. The quotation which has most influenced my thinking and been most helpful to me is from 'My Antonia'.

I was something that lay under the sun and felt it, like the pumpkins, and I did not want to be anything more. I was entirely happy. Perhaps we feel like that when we die and become part of something entire, whether it is sun and air or goodness and knowledge. At any rate, that is happiness, to be dissolved into something complete and great. When it comes to one, it comes as naturally as sleep.

WILLA CATHER

FROM **The Viscount Norwich (John Julius Norwich)**

Writer and broadcaster

I cannot do better than contribute the following passage. Henry Scott Holland was Regius Professor of Theology at Oxford. His dates are 1847 to 1918.

Death is nothing at all . . . I have only slipped away into the next room . . . I am I and you are you . . . whatever we were to each other that we are still. Call me by my old familiar name, speak to me in the easy way which you always used. Put no difference into your tone; wear no forced air of solemnity or sorrow. Laugh as we always laughed at the little jokes we enjoyed together. Play, smile, think of me, pray for me. Let my name be ever the household word that it always was. Let it be spoken without effect, without the ghost of a shadow on it. Life means all that it ever meant. It is the same as it ever was; there is absolutely unbroken continuity. What is death but a negligible accident? Why should I be out of mind because I am out of sight? I am but waiting for you, for an interval, somewhere very near just around the corner . . . All is well.

HENRY SCOTT HOLLAND

FROM **Margaret Torrie**
Founder of Cruse

I have a pearl
  to give to you who weep
  whose beauty's born
  from simple life
  and fashioned out of pain
  it fills a mandala
  with space to breathe
  and gently gathers light
  it is not struck from rock
  or circled like a diamond noose
  to bind you by
  but free and perfect
  grew unknown
  where nature turns invading pain
  to beauty and delight
So hold it fast
  and catch the spread of sunrise
  in the single point of light.

MARGARET TORRIE

Index of Contributors

Index of Sources and Acknowledgements

The compiler acknowledges with gratitude the courtesy of the following companies and individuals in permitting the use of copyright material.

Every endeavour has been made to trace the copyright owners of each extract. There do however remain some extracts for which the source is unknown to the compiler and the publisher. The publisher would be glad to hear from the copyright owners of these extracts and due acknowledgement will be made in all future editions of the book.